GW00367923

A PARRAGON BOOK

Published by Parragon Book Service Ltd,
Units 13-17, Avonbridge Trading Estate, Atlantic Road,
Avonmouth, Bristol BS11 9QD

Produced by The Templar Company plc,
Pippbrook Mill, London Road, Dorking,
Surrey RH4 1JE

Copyright © 1996 Parragon Book Service Limited

Written by Dugald Steer
Series Editor Robert Snedden
Designed by Mark Summersby
All photographs by Neill Bruce Motoring Photolibrary except for
the photo on page 59, courtesy of Andrew Morland.

All rights reserved.

Printed and bound in the UK

ISBN 0 7525 1668 X

FACTFINDERS

FASTEST
CARS

‖ ·PARRAGON· ‖

CONTENTS

INTRODUCTION

The fastest production car in the world
at the moment is the McLaren F1. With
a top speed of just over 230 mph (370
km/h), the technology that has gone
into the car makes it more like a *Grand
Prix* racing car than a typical on-the-
road model. Some people might ask
why anyone would want a car that could
go that fast. There are very few roads in
the world—such as the autobahns in
Germany—that do not have speed lim-
its that are far, far lower than the sort of
speeds that the McLaren can achieve.
And there must be very few people who
are capable of controlling a car that is
travelling that fast. Some might add that
the dangers of this situation are only
highlighted if we consider that a number
of the cars in this book were designed

for Group 4 racing, where on-the-road production cars competed with each other. This class of racing was banned in 1986, after a spate of terrible accidents. Yet people have been fascinated with cars, and how fast they can go, since the very first automobiles, invented by Gottleib Daimler and Karl Benz, appeared just over one hundred years ago. And cars have been getting faster and faster ever since.

In many ways the price of the very fastest cars puts them way beyond the pockets of all but the very rich—a McLaren F1 currently sells for some £634,500, a Jaguar XJ220 for £403,000— yet the exceptional quality of these cars, and the prestige of owning them means that they will always find buyers, although maybe fewer in a recession than at other times. The standard of engineering in high-performance cars tends to be superlative, and techniques developed for top-of-the range supercars eventually find their way back to the ordinary production models, giving an impetus to the more creative side of car building. Also, the cars are usually beautiful, styled by companies such as Pininfarina, Bertone and ItalDesign, who have become almost as famous as the manufacturers they have worked for: Aston Martin, BMW, Ferrari, Jaguar, Lister, Lamborghini, Marcos, Maserati, Porsche and TVR. Just to name them is to conjure up images of wonderfully sleek coupés and open-topped spiders whose engines roar into life as they accelerate off from a standing start and disappear into the distance in a matter of seconds. Even in these days of strict emission regulations and concern for the environment there will be a place for them, and it is difficult to imagine that, in a couple of years, there will not be an on-the-road car that outclasses even the McLaren. Within the pages of this book you will find information about all of these cars—the very fastest production cars ever, masterpieces of steel, aluminium and carbon-fibre that have answered a basic desire for speed and elegance, magnificent road-holding and sometimes even comfort! And though it may be unlikely that we will ever be able to own one we can look, marvel—and dream.

ASTON MARTIN DB7

Engine:	Supercharged straight-6, 3239 cc
Maximum Power:	335 bhp
Length:	463 cm
Width:	182 cm
Transmission:	5-speed manual
Drive:	Rear
Top Speed:	165 mph/265 km/h
Brakes:	Discs with ABS
0-60 mph:	5.8 seconds
Year:	1994
Country Built:	Great Britain

The Aston Martin DB7 was developed to continue the Aston Martin DB series which had been current in the sixties. The initials DB come from Sir David Brown, who had owned Aston Martin from 1947 to 1972. The DB7 was made possible by the fact that Ford, which had owned Aston Martin since 1987, acquired Jaguar in 1989. Jaguar had intended to produce an F-type sports car, as a successor to the E-type, but the project, called Project XX had not been viable. Eventually Project XX became the basis for the DB7, with a supercharged, 3.2-litre version of the Jaguar AJ-6 engine that could produce up to 335 bhp. The car was styled by Ian Callum, who based the look on the style of the DB6. The top speed quoted here was reached in the manufacturer's tests.

The 1993 Aston Martin DB7 pre-production prototype.

ASTON MARTIN VANTAGE ZAGATO

Engine:	Aluminium V-8 four-cam, 5340 cc
Maximum Power:	432 bhp
Length:	439 cm
Width:	187 cm
Transmission:	5-speed manual
Drive:	Rear
Top Speed:	186 mph/299 km/h
Brakes:	Discs
0-60 mph:	4.8 seconds
Year:	1986
Country Built:	Great Britain

The Italian styled Aston Martin Vantage Zagato.

Aston Martin and the Italian styling house of Zagato had at one stage worked together to produce the DB4 Zagato. In 1984, Victor Gauntlet and Peter Livanos of Aston Martin approached the Zagato brothers at the Geneva Motor Show once more. The outcome of this collaboration was to be a new, two-seater model, with a powerful version of the V-8 engine that could generate 432 bhp, reach 60 mph in less than 5 seconds and have a top speed of 300 km/h. A successor to the succesful 170-mph V-8 Vantage was to come later with the Virage and the 1993 Vantage. The Vantage Zagato very nearly achieved its brief, clocking 299 km/h. Eventually all 50 were sold and the company went on to create a slightly slower, open-topped Volante model.

BMW 850CSi

Engine:	Aluminium V-12, 5576 cc
Maximum Power:	380 bhp
Length:	478 cm
Width:	185 cm
Transmission:	6-speed manual
Drive:	Rear
Top Speed:*	170 mph/274 km/h
Brakes:	Discs with ABS
0-60 mph:	5.7 seconds
Year:	1995
Country Built:	Germany

BMW have always tended to have coupés rather than saloons as their top of the range cars and have often tended to use the same parts on different cars in order to save money. The stylish, exclusive 850CSi is the top of the range of a new 8-series which also includes the 840Ci. First launched in 1989, it uses an aluminium V-12 5.6-litre engine which can generate up to 380 bhp. This should take the top speed up to something approaching 170 mph, but BMW now always fit 155 mph speed restrictors to their cars and the top speed which has actually been achieved in the car has been around 156 mph. We have included its potential performance in this book. Acceleration is excellent with 0-60 mph coming up in around 5.7 seconds.

The BMW 850CSi—comfort, speed and luxury.

BMW M1

Engine:	6-cylinder, 3453cc
Maximum Power:	277bhp
Length:	436cm
Width:	183cm
Transmission:	5-speed manual
Drive:	Rear
Top Speed:	162mph/261km/h
Brakes:	Discs
0-60 mph:	5.4 seconds
Year:	1979
Country Built:	Germany

The mid-engined BMW M1—styled in Italy.

Originally designed to take part in Groups 4 and 5 of international sports car racing, the BMW M1 was interesting in that it had a mid-engined layout with the six-cylinder, 3.5-litre engine sitting just behind the driver. The glass-fibre bodywork was designed by the Italian stylist Giugiaro and he eventually ended up taking the car into production jointly with Bauer in Stuttgart when Lamborghini, who had originally been contracted to do the work, had to back out due to financial pressures. 400 BMW M1's were commissioned but, by the time all of them had been completed, changes in the racing rules meant that the M1 never had a proper chance to compete with the Porsches. Still, BMW had produced a supercar that could only enhance their image.

BMW M5

Engine:	6-cylinder, 3795 cc
Maximum Power:	340 bhp
Length:	472 cm
Width:	175 cm
Transmission:	6-speed manual
Drive:	Rear
Top Speed:*	170 mph/274 km/h
Brakes:	Discs with ABS
0-60 mph:	5.4 seconds
Year:	1995
Country Built:	Germany

BMW Motorsport, who had decided to begin producing the M1 in 1976, joined the Brabham *Grand Prix* team and won the championship for the first time in 1983 with Nelson Piquet. As a result of this and of later victories, the names Motorsport and M-power became very well established, and the company started to use them on high performance versions of their road cars. These cars often used the engine that had been developed for the M1. The M5, which first came out in 1985, a year after the general introduction of the 5-series BMW saloons, was no exception. After the M5 came the M3, a version of the 2-door 3-series and, in 1992, the M5 reached its final form with its engine being enlarged to 3.8 litres and tuned to a maximum power output of 340 bhp.

The BMW M5—a saloon that behaves like a sports car.

BUGATTI EB110GT

Engine:	Quad-turbo V-12, 3499 cc
Maximum Power:	553 bhp
Length:	440 cm
Width:	196 cm
Transmission:	6-speed manual
Drive:	Four-wheel
Top Speed:	212 mph/341 km/h
Brakes:	Discs with ABS
0-60 mph:	3.7 seconds
Year:	1993
Country Built:	Italy

The EB110GT—the first major Bugatti for 30 years.

The EB110 was so called because it was launched on the eve of the 110th anniversary of founder Ettore Bugatti's birth. It was the first Bugatti to appear for over 30 years and had been built at a new factory in Campogalliano in Italy. The bodywork was designed by Marcello Gandini, who had worked for Lamborghini, although it was modified by Giampaolo Benedini when Bugatti chairman Romano Artioli decided he was not entirely happy with it. The chassis was of carbon-fibre and the car was powered by a mid-located V-12 engine. At the end of 1993 the EB110 was renamed the EB110GT and the EB110SS was introduced. Generating more than 600 bhp, it was claimed that this impressive car had a top speed of 217 mph and a 0-60 mph figure of a mere 3.4 seconds.

CHEVROLET CORVETTE ZR-1

Engine:	Aluminium 4-cam, V-8, 5727 cc
Maximum Power:	380 bhp
Length:	448 cm
Width:	180 cm
Transmission:	6-speed manual
Drive:	Rear
Top Speed:	172 mph/277 km/h
Brakes:	Discs with ABS
0-60 mph:	5.1 seconds
Year:	1989
Country Built:	USA

The first Chevrolet Corvette was produced in 1953 and the ZR-1, which was introduced in 1989, became the latest in a long line of Corvettes. Its style and glass-fibre bodywork was the same as that of the 1983 Corvette model, which had been styled by Chevrolet's Jerry Palmer, but the engine had much more power having been specially designed in alloy by Lotus. This new four-cam four-valve 5.7-litre engine gave the car a maximum power output of 380 bhp and a top speed of around 172 mph. Other modifications were the addition of ABS brakes and a six-speed gearbox. The car remained relatively cheap for a fast sports car which could offer such high performance levels and had a price-tag in the region of a mere $50,000.

The Chevrolet Corvette ZR-1—an American supercar.

CHRYSLER VIPER

Engine:	Aluminium V-10, 7990 cc
Maximum Power:	406 bhp
Length:	445 cm
Width:	192 cm
Transmission:	6-speed manual
Drive:	Rear
Top Speed:	167 mph/269 km/h
Brakes:	Discs
0-60 mph:	4.6 seconds
Year:	1993
Country Built:	USA

The Chrysler Viper—a fast car with retro appeal.

The Chrysler Viper, known in the United States as the Dodge Viper, has a retro appeal that makes it reminiscent of some of the famous 'sixties sports cars such as the 160-mph AC Cobra. Indeed the Chrysler president, Bob Lutz, employed Carroll Shelby, the Cobra's original creator, to help him in the design of the Viper. Although it was not designed specifically for production, the car was first shown at the North American Auto Show in January 1989, and there was such interest that it was launched as a road car in 1991. The show model's V-10 engine, originally a cast-iron truck unit, had been re-engineered by Lamborghini in aluminium to develop up to 406 bhp. It can accelerate very quickly in any gear and, in 1993, a coupé version was launched.

FERRARI 288GTO

Engine:	Aluminium V-8 twin turbo, 2855 cc
Maximum Power:	400 bhp
Length:	429 cm
Width:	191 cm
Transmission:	5-speed manual
Drive:	Rear
Top Speed:	189 mph/304 km/h
Brakes:	Discs
0-60 mph:	5 seconds
Year:	1986
Country Built:	Italy

The Ferrari 288GTO was designed to compete in Group B racing but the rules stated that a required number of cars had to be built. Group B racing, which was very dangerous, was banned in 1986. As a result the 288GTO was never used for racing but still became a classic sports car, with a top speed of around 186 mph. The name GTO was taken from the Ferrari racing 250GTO of the 'fifties and stood for *Gran Turismo Omologato*. *Omologato* is the Italian for "homologated" and this means that a number of cars are certified as having been made. The design of the car was based on the Ferrari 308GTB but it was a little longer and wider, with bodywork of glass-fibre, Kevlar and carbon-fibre. Production of the car ceased in 1986 by which time 273 had been built.

A 1984 Ferrari 288GTO—note the wrong numberplate!

FERRARI F355

Engine:	Aluminium V-8, 3496 cc
Maximum Power:	380 bhp
Length:	425 cm
Width:	194 cm
Transmission:	6-speed manual
Drive:	Rear
Top Speed:	183 mph/293 km/h
Brakes:	Discs with ABS
0-60 mph:	4.6 seconds
Year:	1995
Country Built:	Italy

A Ferrari F355 Berlinetta at Goodwood.

The origins of the Ferrari F355 Berlinetta, GTS and open-topped Spider begin with an engine Ferrari originally designed and which Fiat built and installed in their front-engined Fiat Dino in the 'sixties. The collaboration came about because enough cars needed to be built with the engine for Ferrari to race with it in Formula 2 and Ferrari used it in their rear-engined Ferrari Dino 246. The Dino's successor, the 308GT4, used a larger 3-litre V-8 engine and, over the years, the engine size increased with each model change. The 355, which came out in 1994, has a 3.5-litre engine which can generate up to 375 bhp, which is remarkable given that it does not have turbochargers. This allows it a top speed of 183 mph and a rate of acceleration of 0-60 mph in less than 5 seconds.

FERRARI 365GTB/4 DAYTONA

Engine:	Aluminium V-12, 4390cc
Maximum Power:	352 bhp
Length:	442 cm
Width:	176 cm
Transmission:	5-speed manual
Drive:	Rear
Top Speed:	174 mph/280 km/h
Brakes:	Discs
0-60 mph:	5.4 seconds
Year:	1971
Country Built:	Italy

The most striking thing visually about the Ferrari 365GTB/4 was its chiselled front end, two-door body and truncated tail magnificently designed by the Italian styling house of Pininfarina. It became the fastest car of its day due to its top speed of 174 mph and was first exhibited at the Paris Motor Show in 1968. The previous year a Ferrari 365GTB/4 had won the Daytona 24-hour race in America, and soon the name of the race had become for ever associated with the car. It had a steel body with doors, bonnet and boot lid of aluminium. Initially, its four headlights were contained behind plexiglass covers. Although not designed as a race car, the Daytona had various successes at Le Mans. In 1969 an open-topped version was introduced—the 365GTS/4.

The open-topped Daytona Spider 365GTS/4.

FERRARI 410 SUPERAMERICA

Engine:	Aluminium V-12, 4962 cc
Maximum Power:	360 bhp
Length:	467 cm
Width:	178 cm
Transmission:	4-speed manual
Drive:	Rear
Top Speed:	165 mph/265 km/h
Brakes:	Drums
0-60 mph:	6.6 seconds
Year:	1959
Country Built:	Italy

The Ferrari 410 Superamerica—a lot of power for 1959.

With a top speed of around 165 mph, the Ferrari 410 Superamerica was an extremely fast car for 1959, being powered by a 4.9-litre V-12 engine that could produce 360 bhp. The name 410 Superamerica came partially from the fact that the car was designed mainly for the American market, and partially from the fact that many Ferrari model names are based on the capacity of a single cylinder. Each of the 12 cylinders in the 410 Superamerica had a cubic capacity of 413.5 cc, which was near enough to "410". As was usual with Ferrari road cars the body was styled by the Pininfarina styling house. The engine was a big, 4.9-litre V-12 designed for Ferrari by Lampredi to take into account the fast, high horsepower figures needed to attract the Americans.

FERRARI 456GT

Engine:	Aluminium V-12, 5474 cc
Maximum Power:	442 bhp
Length:	473 cm
Width:	192 cm
Transmission:	6-speed manual
Drive:	Rear
Top Speed:	187 mph/301 km/h
Brakes:	Discs with ABS
0-60 mph:	5.1 seconds
Year:	1994
Country Built:	Italy

Designed to recall the 1960's Daytona in style, the Ferrari 456GT is unusual for a Ferrari in that it is a comfortable four-seater which has again been named after the capacity of a single cylinder—in this case 456 cc. It was the last Ferrari that company founder Enzo Ferrari was involved with before his death and it was styled by Pininfarina, as so many Ferraris have been, and costs something in the region of £156,500. The powerful V-12 engine, which can develop up to 442 bhp, is located at the front of the car, rather than in the middle, and the car can accelerate to 60 mph in 5.1 seconds, has excellent brakes and a truly luxurious interior. The company claim that it will do up to 187 mph even loaded with people and luggage and it has had a great reception.

The Ferrari 456GT—a Daytona for the 'nineties.

FERRARI 512M

Engine:	Aluminium flat-12, 4943 cc
Maximum Power:	422 bhp
Length:	448 cm
Width:	198 cm
Transmission:	5-speed manual
Drive:	Rear
Top Speed:	192 mph/309 km/h
Brakes:	Discs with ABS
0-60 mph:	4.8 seconds
Year:	1995
Country Built:	Italy

The Ferrari 512M.

The Ferrari 512M can trace its development back to the 1973 Berlinetta Boxer, the 365GT4BB, which was launched as early as 1971. The Boxer, as it became known, was styled by Pininfarina, as was its successor the 1984 Testarossa. Testarossa means "redhead" in Italian, the name coming from the car's red cam covers. The car's most distinctive feature was its radiator intakes, which were mounted behind the doors with the grille pattern being continued along them. The Testarossa was eventually replaced, in 1992, by the 512TR, whose 5-litre flat-6 engine could generate 428 bhp. The 512TR had a top speed of 188 mph. The lighter 512M came out not long afterwards and is capable of 0-60 mph in 4.8 seconds. It has a top speed of 192 mph.

FERRARI F50

Engine:	Aluminium V-12, 4698 cc
Maximum Power:	513 bhp
Length:	448 cm
Width:	199 cm
Transmission:	5-speed manual
Drive:	Rear
Top Speed:	202 mph/325 km/h
Brakes:	Discs
0-60 mph:	3.7 seconds
Year:	1995
Country Built:	Italy

The Ferrari F40 was launched in 1987 to celebrate 40 years of Ferrari cars and it became the fastest car of its day, overtaking the Porsche 959. The car's bodywork, with its distinctive rear spoiler, was styled by Pininfarina and the body was built almost totally of Kevlar and carbon-fibre, making it very light and very strong. Extensive wind tunnel testing made sure the car had a very low drag factor. It had three drive heights that could be selected and it had a top speed of 198 mph, with its 2.9-litre V-8 twin-turbo engine producing up to 478 bhp. In 1995 came the F40's successor, the F50. With even better roadholding than the F40 this car has a 4.7-litre V-8 engine, can accelerate from 0-60 in 3.7 seconds, generates 513 bhp and has a top speed of over 200 mph.

The Ferrari F50—Ferrari approaches its 50th birthday.

FORD GT40 MkIII

Engine:	Cast iron V-8, 4727 cc
Maximum Power:	306 bhp
Length:	429 cm
Width:	178 cm
Transmission:	5-speed manual
Drive:	Rear
Top Speed:	164 mph/264 km/h
Brakes:	Discs
0-60 mph:	5.3 seconds
Year:	1966
Country Built:	Great Britain

The Ford GT40 MkIII—road version of a racer.

During the 1960's the Ford Motor Company became interested in appealing to younger drivers. It developed the sporty, 111-mph Ford Mustang, but, as Ford had long been associated with cheap, sensible family cars it also realised that it needed to raise its sports profile in order to sell such cars. Deciding to develop a sports car to race at Le Mans, Ford worked with a British company, Lola Cars, who had used Ford engines successfully in the past. The result was the Ford GT40, so called because the original car was 40 inches high. The GT40's failed to finish in the 1964 Le Mans race, but the Mark II's came first, second and third the following year. A detuned road-going version, the Mark III, became available from 1966, but very few were ever actually built.

HONDA NSX-T

Engine:	Aluminium V-6, 2977 cc
Maximum Power:	270 bhp
Length:	443 cm
Width:	181 cm
Transmission:	5-speed manual
Drive:	Rear
Top Speed:	166 mph/267 km/h
Brakes:	Discs with ABS
0-60 mph:	6.5 seconds
Year:	1995
Country Built:	Japan

Honda, the world's largest producer of motorcycles, first became a car manufacturer in 1962 and enjoyed *Grand Prix* victories in Mexico and Italy. But it was during the mid 'eighties that the company decided that it needed a showcase supercar to lead its range and rival the cars that were being produced by Ferrari and Porsche. The Japanese certainly had the technology available, and work first began on the NSX in 1984. Eventually it was launched in 1989 and production began in 1990. The car's bodywork was almost entirely aluminium, which made it very light, while its engine was a V-6 that could generate up to 270 bhp. The car had a top speed of 160 mph. In 1995 the open-topped Honda NSX-T was introduced, only unusual in that it is even faster than the NSX.

The Honda NSX—a showcase for Japanese technology.

ISDERA IMPERATOR 108i

Engine:	Aluminium V-8, 5547 cc
Maximum Power:	390 bhp
Length:	422 cm
Width:	183 cm
Transmission:	5-speed manual
Drive:	Rear
Top Speed:	176 mph/283 km/h
Brakes:	Discs
0-60 mph:	5.0 seconds
Year:	1987
Country Built:	Germany

The Isdera Imperator 108i—German engineering.

The Isdera Imperator 108i was the brainchild of
Eberhard Schultz, who moved from working at Porsche
to opening his own engineering consultancy in 1981. A
number of cars have been built by the company in
addition to their other work. Mercedes engines have been
used and the first cars to be introduced in 1983 were the
open-topped Spyder 033i and the 036i—the difference
between the models being the engine used. The design of
the Isdera Imperator, which came out in 1984, was based
on a 1978 design study for Mercedes—the CW311, and
this was updated for the latest 1991 model. The car used
a V-8 engine from the Mercedes SL500, which was
boosted to provide 390 bhp. The latest Isdera is the
Commendatore 112i, whose engine can produce 408 bhp.

Iso Grifo GL365

Engine:	Cast iron V-8, 5360 cc
Maximum Power:	365 bhp
Length:	444 cm
Width:	177 cm
Transmission:	4-speed manual
Drive:	Rear
Top Speed:	161 mph/259 km/h
Brakes:	Discs
0-60 mph:	7.4 seconds
Year:	1966
Country Built:	Italy

The Iso Rivolta was launched in 1963 at the Geneva Motor Show. Its creation was the result of Count Renzo Rivolta's determination that the Milan based Iso company should build a GT car for the luxury market. The car was built by Bertone, closely following an earlier design by stylist Giorgetto Giugiaro for the Gordon GT—the car that became the 135-mph Gordon Keeble. A year later the slightly shorter Iso Grifo was launched in two versions—the on-the-road Luxury A3L and the racing Competition A3C which came 14th in the 1964 Le Mans race, and 9th in the race of 1965. The standard Iso Grifo A3L engine was a 365 bhp version of a Chevrolet V-8 and, as a result, the car became known as the Iso Grifo GL365. It was in production until 1974.

The Iso Grifo GL365—Italian style, American engine.

JAGUAR D-TYPE

Engine:	Straight 6, 3442 cc
Maximum Power:	250 bhp
Length:	410 cm
Width:	166 cm
Transmission:	4-speed manual
Drive:	Rear
Top Speed:	162 mph/261 km/h
Brakes:	Discs
0-60 mph:	4.7 seconds
Year:	1956
Country Built:	Great Britain

A Jaguar D-type long-nose.

Although the Jaguar D-type, which came out in the mid 'fifties, was first and foremost designed to be a racing car, a number of customers licensed their cars for on-the-road use. Also, a specific on-the-road version, the XKSS, went into production although very few of them were ever actually built. The beautiful, aerodynamic bodywork on the Jaguar D-type was designed by Malcolm Sayer and the car used a 3.4-litre XK engine that could produce up to 250 bhp, giving the car a top speed of 162 mph. There were two versions produced—a long-nose, which was primarily used for racing, and an earlier short-nose, which was the type that was sold to customers. The famous E-type, which replaced the D-type, was first introduced in 1961.

JAGUAR XJ220

Engine:	Twin turbo V-6, 3498 cc
Maximum Power:	549 bhp
Length:	493 cm
Width:	222 cm
Transmission:	5-speed manual
Drive:	Rear
Top Speed:	217 mph/349 km/h
Brakes:	Discs
0-60 mph:	3.6 seconds
Year:	1993
Country Built:	Great Britain

The development of the XJ220 began in 1984. It was originally designed as a four-wheel-drive car with a 500-bhp V-12 engine that would be suitable for Group 4 racing. The prototype was launched in 1988 at the Birmingham Motor Show and, after the show, it was decided that the car would be produced by Jaguar Sport using a turbocharged 3.5-litre V-6 engine instead of the V-12. This engine was able to produce up to 550 bhp. The chassis was also changed—using aluminium honeycomb rather than sheet aluminium, which helped to make the car lighter. Deliveries were scheduled to take place by early 1992 and, by then, the XJ220 was the fastest and most expensive car in the world, only to be outdone by the Bugatti EB110SS and the McLaren F1.

The No 1 production Jaguar XJ220.

LAMBORGHINI COUNTACH

Engine:	Aluminium V-12, 5167 cc
Maximum Power:	455 bhp
Length:	414 cm
Width:	199 cm
Transmission:	5-speed manual
Drive:	Rear
Top Speed:	190 mph/306 km/h
Brakes:	Discs
0-60 mph:	4.9 seconds
Year:	1986
Country Built:	Italy

The Lamborghini Countach with its doors up.

The Lamborghini Countach was launched in 1971 and
production began in 1974. The car was mid-engined, but
the engine was mounted longitudinally and the gearbox
was situated at the front of the car, giving good weight
distribution and a very smooth gear change. Its name, the
Countach, is a word used to express amazed delight in
the Turin Italian dialect. Initially the car was known as
the LP500, because of the size of its 5-litre V-12 engine,
but this was reduced to 4 litres for the actual production
model, the LP400. Over the 16 years that the Countach
was in production there were various model changes. In
1986 the engine was enlarged to 5.2 litres to produce the
LP5000QV. Maximum speed tests on the car varied
between 180 and 190 mph and production ceased in 1990.

LAMBORGHINI DIABLO

Engine:	Aluminium V-12, 5707 cc
Maximum Power:	492 bhp
Length:	446 cm
Width:	204 cm
Transmission:	5-speed manual
Drive:	Rear
Top Speed:	205 mph/330 km/h
Brakes:	Discs
0-60 mph:	4.4 seconds
Year:	1994
Country Built:	Italy

Design work on the Lamborghini Diablo was started in 1986. Marcello Gandini worked on the bodywork with some input from Chrysler, Lamborghini's then owners. Its shape was more aerodynamic than the Countach, and its mid-located V-12 engine was enlarged to 5.7 litres. The Diablo, or "Devil", was named after a famous fighting bull and was launched in 1990. Initially the car came in a rear-wheel-drive format, without either power-assisted steering or ABS brakes but later the four-wheel-drive open-topped Diablo VT was launched and then, in September 1993, the Diablo 30SE, which had both power-assisted steering and ABS. The power of the engine was boosted to 525 bhp and the weight was reduced, giving it a top speed of nearly 220 mph.

The Lamborghini Diablo—designed to tempt.

LAMBORGHINI MIURA

Engine:	Aluminium V-12, 3929 cc
Maximum Power:	370 bhp
Length:	432 cm
Width:	175 cm
Transmission:	5-speed manual
Drive:	Rear
Top Speed:	172 mph/277 km/h
Brakes:	Discs
0-60 mph:	6.7 seconds
Year:	1970
Country Built:	Italy

The Lamborghini Miura SV.

Ferruccio Lamborghini set out to build luxury GT cars in the early 'sixties and his first car was the 350GT of 1963. Ferruccio now continued to develop another car— initially known as the 400GT. A new 3.9-litre V-12 engine was created which was situated behind the passenger compartment and, to save space, was mounted transversely with the gearbox underneath it—like the British Mini. The body of the car was designed by Marcello Gandini and the car was a great success at the Geneva Motor Show in 1966. The Lamborghini insignia was a bull and the car was named after a breed of fighting bull. The first Miuras were delivered in 1967 and from then on the car was modified to create the 370 bhp Miura P400S in 1969, and the SV in 1970.

LISTER STORM

Engine:	Aluminium V-12, 6996 cc
Maximum Power:	594 bhp
Length:	455 cm
Width:	198 cm
Transmission:	6-speed manual
Drive:	Rear
Top Speed:	200 mph/322 km/h
Brakes:	Discs with ABS
0-60 mph:	4.1 seconds
Year:	1995
Country Built:	Great Britain

Lister Cars, which is currently based in Leatherhead in Surrey and owned by Laurence Pearce, is named after Brian Lister, who built a number of racing Lister Jaguar cars in the 'fifties. The latest Lister car, the Lister Storm, was launched at the Earls Court Motorshow in 1993 and the first production model was bought by the incredibly wealthy Sultan of Brunei. The car is front-engined, which is not common among supercars these days, and it has quite a lot of space in its boot for luggage. It is also the most roomy and comfortable of its supercar rivals, the McLaren F1, Bugatti EB110 and Jaguar XJ220. Its 7-litre Jaguar V-12 engine uses two superchargers and produces up to 594 bhp, giving the car an exceptional top speed of some 200 mph.

The Lister Storm at Denbies Wine Estate, Dorking.

LOTUS ESPRIT SPORT 300

Engine:	Turbo 4-cylinder, 2174 cc
Maximum Power:	306 bhp
Length:	439 cm
Width:	191 cm
Transmission:	5-speed manual
Drive:	Rear
Top Speed:	161 mph/259 km/h
Brakes:	Discs with ABS
0-60 mph:	4.7 seconds
Year:	1993
Country Built:	Great Britain

The Lotus Esprit Sport S4.

The Lotus Esprit was launched in 1975 and, in 1976, the first cars were delivered. Styled by Giorgetto Giugiaro's company ItalDesign, the car had a mid-mounted, 2-litre engine which gave it 160 bhp and a top speed of around 125 mph. In 1980 this model was joined by the Esprit Turbo, which used a 2.2-litre engine fitted with turbochargers to take the maximum power to 210 bhp and its top speed to 150 mph. In 1993 the Sport 300 was launched—its bigger turbochargers, better suspension and wider wheels gave it 306 bhp and a top speed of 161 mph. A much more comfortable version, the S4 was also launched as the standard model and the SVS, which combined the comfort of the S4 with most of the performance of the Sport 300, came out in 1994.

MARCOS LM500 COUPÉ

Engine:	Aluminium V-8, 4995 cc
Maximum Power:	350 bhp
Length:	426 cm
Width:	183 cm
Transmission:	5-speed manual
Drive:	Rear
Top Speed:	170 mph/272 km/h
Brakes:	Discs
0-60 mph:	4.2 seconds
Year:	1993
Country Built:	Great Britain

After a number of years without producing any cars, Marcos launched the Marcos Mantula in 1981. This car used a 4-litre Rover V-8 engine in a steel chassis and a number of cars were to follow. The Mantara came out in 1993 and, later that year, a GT racing car—the GT LeMans—was released. The Marcos LM 500 is a roadgoing version of this car, with a 5-litre Rover V-8 engine that can generate up to 320 bhp. The car has a top speed of 170 mph and is available in both open-topped Spider and Coupé forms. In 1985 the Mantara LM 600 was launched. Here, the engine has been expanded to 6 litres producing a massive 460 bhp. Its estimated top speed is around 185 mph and it can accelerate from 0-60 mph in 3.9 seconds.

The Marcos LM500 Coupé.

MASERATI SHAMAL

Engine:	Aluminium V-8, 3217 cc
Maximum Power:	326 bhp
Length:	410 cm
Width:	185 cm
Transmission:	6-speed manual
Drive:	Rear
Top Speed:	168 mph/269 km/h
Brakes:	Discs
0-60 mph:	5.1 seconds
Year:	1992
Country Built:	Italy

The Maserati company, which was founded in 1926, has a tradition of naming some of its high performance cars after powerful winds from around the world. The Ghibli, the Bora and the Merak are a few of the names that have been used. The Maserati Shamal, which was launched in 1992, is no exception and it is named after the hot, dry wind that sweeps across the countries of Iran and Iraq in June and July. Its basic shape originated with the 1982 Maserati Biturbo and 1984 Spyder, and it was developed at the time when Maserati were owned by De Tomaso. The Maserati Shamal uses a 3.2-litre engine and twin turbochargers to generate 326 bhp, it has a top speed of some 168 mph and can accelerate from 0-60 mph in just over 5 seconds.

The Maserati Shamal—rides like the wind.

McLaren F1

Engine:	Aluminium V-12, 6064cc
Maximum Power:	627bhp
Length:	429 m
Width:	183 m
Transmission:	6-speed manual
Drive:	Rear
Top Speed:	231mph/370 km/h
Brakes:	Discs
0-60 mph:	3.2 seconds
Year:	1994
Country Built:	Great Britain

With its Grand Prix technology the McLaren F1 was designed for use on the road to be the fastest, most agile production car ever made and its top speed of over 230 mph and acceleration from 0-60 mph in just over 3 seconds mean that it is a truly remarkable car. Gordon Murray worked on the technical side, whereas Peter Stevens, who had earlier designed the lines of the Lotus Elan and Jaguar XJR-15, worked on styling. Work began on the car in 1989. Every part of the car was created from scratch especially for the car, from the 6.1-litre V-12 engine, made specially by BMW, to the chassis and body-work, which incorporated a great deal of carbon-fibre. All this also makes the car the most expensive ever—it currently costs £634,500 before tax.

The McLaren F1 pre-production prototype.

MERCEDES-BENZ SL600

Engine:	Aluminium V-12, 5987 cc
Maximum Power:	389 bhp
Length:	447 cm
Width:	181 cm
Transmission:	Automatic
Drive:	Rear
Top Speed:*	168 mph/270 km/h
Brakes:	Discs with ABS
0-60 mph:	5.9 seconds
Year:	1992
Country Built:	Germany

There have been various Mercedes-Benz SL, or Sports Light, cars since the company won Le Mans in 1952 with their 300SL coupé. The latest group of SL's came out in 1989—they have a hard top that can be added to them which has the effect of increasing acceleration. The cars in this series are very much showcases of technology, with all sorts of safety gadgets such as roll-bars which come up automatically if the car's on-board sensors detect that a roll-over may be about to happen. The top of the range is the SL600, which was introduced in 1992, and which uses a 6-litre engine to produce a maximum power output of 389 bhp. This should give a top speed of at least 165 mph, but Mercedes, like BMW, have installed limiters on their cars which allow them a maximum of 155 mph.

The Mercedes-Benz SL600 with removable hard top.

PORSCHE 911 CARRERA RS

Engine:	Air cooled flat-6, 3746 cc
Maximum Power:	260 bhp
Length:	425 cm
Width:	174 cm
Transmission:	5-speed manual
Drive:	Rear
Top Speed:	172 mph/275 km/h
Brakes:	Discs
0-60 mph:	4.9 seconds
Year:	1991
Country Built:	Germany

The rear-engined Porsche 911 first came out in 1963. Its 2-litre, 130-bhp flat-6 engine and superb aerodynamic shape gave it a top speed approaching 130 mph. Apart from a slight weight problem at the back of the car that could make cornering at speed difficult it has remained an exceptional car for more than 30 years. The engine capacity has gradually increased until today the 3.8-litre 911 Carrera RS is a coupé which can develop up to 300 bhp and, it is claimed, travel at up to 172 mph. This top speed has been greatly helped by the fact that the latest model of the Carrera RS is lighter than earlier models. Other recent models include the four-wheel-drive 1994 3.6-litre Carrera 4 and the open-topped 1995 3.8-litre Targa, which has a retractable roof-section.

The Porsche 911 Carrera RS has a thirty-year history.

PORSCHE 911 CARRERA TURBO

Engine:	Turbocharged flat-6, 3600 cc
Maximum Power:	360 bhp
Length:	425 cm
Width:	177 cm
Transmission:	5-speed manual
Drive:	Four-wheel
Top Speed:	180 mph/288 km/h
Brakes:	Discs with ABS
0-60 mph:	4.6 seconds
Year:	1995
Country Built:	Germany

The Porsche 911 Turbo was launched in 1975—developed for Group 4 racing it had to be a production road car and 400 had to be built before it could race. The Turbo was more luxurious than the standard 911 with a large spoiler at the back and wider tyres. The first production model had a 3-litre engine whose 260 bhp took it up to around 155 mph. In 1977 the engine size was increased to 3.3 litres, developing 300 bhp and 162 mph and later, in 1990, 320 bhp and 167 mph. In 1992 there was another increase to 3.6 litres. The most recent, four-wheel-drive, model, the 1995 911 Carrera Turbo, with special hollow spokes to reduce wheel weight, uses a 3.6-litre Carrera engine to generate a massive 408 bhp, and has a top speed of around 180 mph.

The four-wheel drive Porsche 911 Carrera Turbo.

PORSCHE 928GTS 5.4

Engine:	Aluminium V-8, 5397 cc
Maximum Power:	360 bhp
Length:	452 cm
Width:	189 cm
Transmission:	5-speed manual
Drive:	Rear
Top Speed:	168 mph/270 km/h
Brakes:	Discs with ABS
0-60 mph:	5.4 seconds
Year:	1992
Country Built:	Germany

The development of the Porsche 928 began in 1971 and the car was at first thought of as a spacious, front-engined, GT-style replacement for the 911. The 911 did not die, but the 928 certainly carved out a niche for itself, becoming Car of the Year in 1978, a year after its launch. The 1977 model had a new 4.5-litre V-8 engine that could produce 240 bhp. It had a top speed of 140 mph. Much of its body was of aluminium and its bumpers were hidden behind deformable plastic which could spring back into perfect shape after a minor accident. Over the years Porsche improved the model, increasing the capacity of the engine until the 1992 928GTS had a capacity of 5.4 litres, generating 350 bhp, a rate of acceleration from 0-60 mph of 5.4 seconds and a top speed of 168 mph.

The Porsche 928GTS—Car of the Year in 1978.

PORSCHE 959

Engine:	Aluminium flat-6 twin turbo, 2850 cc
Maximum Power:	450 bhp
Length:	424 cm
Width:	193 cm
Transmission:	6-speed manual
Drive:	Four-wheel
Top Speed:	197 mph/317 km/h
Brakes:	Discs with ABS
0-60 mph:	3.7 seconds
Year:	1985
Country Built:	Germany

The Porsche 959 was based on the long-running 911 and it became the fastest Porsche ever made. Initially the idea had been to create a new four-wheel-drive car for Group B racing, and only 200 959's needed to be produced for the car to qualify. In 1981, a four-wheel-drive 911 had been exhibited then, in 1983, the 959 was launched—although none would actually be delivered until 1987. The car had a 2.8-litre flat-6 engine with the most powerful twin turbochargers ever attached to a road car. Its output of 450 bhp could take it up to 167 mph and, along with four-wheel-drive it had many new features, such as adjustable ride height. Unfortunately, Group B was banned in 1986, but a prototype won the Paris-Dakkar Rally in 1984 and a 959 won it in 1986.

A 1988 Porsche 959 Competition Version.

RENAULT ALPINE A610 TURBO

Engine:	Turbocharged V-6, 2975 cc
Maximum Power:	250 bhp
Length:	444 cm
Width:	175 cm
Transmission:	5-speed manual
Drive:	Rear
Top Speed:	161 mph/259 km/h
Brakes:	Discs with ABS
0-60 mph:	5.8 seconds
Year:	1992
Country Built:	France

Alpine have had a long association with Renault and they have used Renault engines to power their racing and performance cars since the very first Alpine, the A106 of 1955. Gradually, Renault came to own more and more of Alpine until the company became, effectively, their competition department. The partnership has always been fruitful. The glass-fibre-bodied Renault Alpine A610 Turbo was a classic example of this partnership, although its production life only lasted from 1991 to 1994. The car's predecessors were the 1980 A310 and 1985 GTA. These front-wheel-drive cars had their engines mounted behind the rear axle in the same way as the A610, but the A610 used a more powerful, turbocharged, 3-litre Peugeot-Renault-Volvo engine.

The Renault Alpine A610 Turbo—a French supercar.

TVR GRIFFITH 500

Engine:	Aluminium V-8, 4997 cc
Maximum Power:	340 bhp
Length:	389 cm
Width:	194 cm
Transmission:	5-speed manual
Drive:	Rear
Top Speed:	161 mph/259 km/h
Brakes:	Discs
0-60 mph:	4.2 seconds
Year:	1993
Country Built:	Great Britain

The initials "TVR" come from the name of Trevor Wilkinson, TVR's founder who, in 1949, began to produce sports cars, using Ford engines to power them. The company is currently owned by Peter Wheeler. The TVR Griffith, which was launched in 1992, is built in Blackpool and its name recalls a number of Griffith cars that were built during the 'sixties. The 1992 TVR Griffith was an open-topped, on-the-road version of TVR's successful Tuscan racing cars and it used a 4.3-litre Rover engine that could produce up to 280 bhp. The car had a soft top that was notable for being very quick and easy to open. The current version of the Griffith is the Griffith 500, which has a 5-litre engine, develops up to 340 bhp and has very rapid acceleration.

The stylish TVR Griffith 500.

VAUXHALL LOTUS CARLTON

Engine:	Turbo straight-6, 3638 cc
Maximum Power:	377 bhp
Length:	477 cm
Width:	193 cm
Transmission:	6-speed manual
Drive:	Rear
Top Speed:	173 mph/278 km/h
Brakes:	Discs with ABS
0-60 mph:	5.3 seconds
Year:	1990
Country Built:	Great Britain

Between 1986 and 1994 Norfolk based Lotus were owned by General Motors and it was during this time that the Lotus Carlton—which was also sold as the Opel Lotus Omega—was developed to be a showcase for Lotus Engineering. Unfortunately, although this was an exceptional car, it may well be that its name, associating it with Vauxhall and Opel, led it to have a much shorter production life than it might have had if it had been a BMW or a Mercedes. It was in production for just over two years. The basis of the car was a Carlton 3.0 GSi whose engine capacity was increased to 3.6 litres. Two turbochargers were also added and this gave the car a maximum power output of 377 bhp. The Vauxhall Lotus Carlton is the fastest ever 5-seater car.

The Vauxhall Lotus Carlton—a 5-seater supercar.

VENTURI 400GT

Engine:	Aluminium V-6 twin-turbo, 2975 cc
Maximum Power:	408 bhp
Length:	414 cm
Width:	199 cm
Transmission:	5-speed manual
Drive:	Rear
Top Speed:	175 mph/281 km/h
Brakes:	Discs
0-60 mph:	4.7 seconds
Year:	1995
Country Built:	France

The French company of Venturi was founded in 1984 with the intention of producing performance cars and, like Alpine, has used engines that were developed by Renault. They produce luxurious performance cars, whose interiors feature leather and polished wood veneer panels. The company's first car was the 2.5-litre 210 and their second the 260. This used a 2.85-litre V-6, producing 260 bhp. This car also came in a specially lightened format, the Atlantique, and could do 165 mph. A Venturi 400 was developed for the amateur Gentleman Drivers Trophy. With a 3-litre V-6 engine it used twin-turbos to produce 408 bhp. The car was successful and so a road-going version, the 400GT was produced. At the moment this is the only current French supercar.

The Venturi 400GT—the only current French supercar.

CAR SPECIFICATIONS

Name: The cars in this book are listed in alphabetical order by make (e.g Ferrari) and then model number or name (e.g. 365GTB/4 Daytona).

Engine: All the cars in this book use petrol-driven engines which may be turbocharged or supercharged. The engine capacity is given in cubic centimetres (cc), and represents the capacity of a single cylinder with the piston at the bottom of its stroke multiplied by the number of cylinders.

Maximum Power: The figure given is the maximum power generated by the engine when it was tested in brake horse-power (bhp). The testing device used is known as a dynamometer and testing has usually been done by the manufacturer.

Length: The overall length of the cars is given. The figure is given in centimetres (cm) and includes such things as front and rear bumpers.

Width: The overall width of the cars is given in centimetres (cm).

Transmission: There are various types of transmission—most of the cars in this book have manual transmission with between four and six gears, although a few are either automatic, or automatic versions of the cars are available (which tends to be essential for the American market).

Drive: Cars can be front-wheel-drive, rear-wheel-drive or four-wheel-drive and this is indicated.

Top Speed: The figure is given in both miles per hour (mph) and kilometres per hour (km/h). By and large the figures given are those achieved in independant tests but in a few instances manufacturer's figures have been used. For the most recent BMW's and the Mercedes-Benz 600SL, which have electronic restrictors fitted to limit the actual top speed that the car may achieve, the potential top speed of the car has been estimated. These cases have been marked with a star (*) to highlight them.

Brakes: The type of brakes that the car uses—almost all of the cars in this book have disc brakes on all four wheels, rather than drum brakes, and many of them use an anti-lock braking system (ABS).

0-60 mph: The time is given in seconds to one decimal place. When cars are tested, the best figure from a number of trials is taken. They accelerate from standstill to an electronically measured speed, in this case 60 mph. In a way this is an arbitrary figure.

Year: If at all possible, the year in which the car was tested is given, or else the data are applicable to a car of that year.

Country Built: Where companies from more than one country have been involved in the development of a car, we have listed the country where the car was actually constructed.

TOP SPEEDS (MPH)

McLaren F1	231
Bugatti EB110S	218
Jaguar XJ220	217
Bugatti EB110GT	212
Lamborghini Diablo SE	207
Lamborghini Diablo	205
Lamborghini Diablo VT	202
Ferrari F50	202
Lister Storm V12	200
Ferrari F40	198
Porsche 959	197
Ferrari 512M	192
Lamborghini Countach QV5000	190
Ferrari 288GTO	189
Ferrari 512TR	188
Ferrari 456GT	187
Aston Martin Vantage Zagato	186
Aston Martin Vantage (1993)	184
Ferrari F355 Berlinetta	183
Ferrari F355 GTS	183
Ferrari F355 Spider	183